Everything the Light Touches

I wanted to give you a book full of hope. So, when I first
wrote it, I focused on what I thought people wanted to hear.
I left out all my pain and the depth that each experience had
given me. I made sure to keep it light and airy. So, it was
no surprise when my first draft lacked authenticity and
became shallow, nauseating, and cliché. I needed to dig
deeper and accept that part of my experience was dark.
But darkness is not harmful, it is just a different wavelength
of beauty, and it is so rich that the eyes cannot perceive it. I
realized that what may seem dark in visible light is bright
in other places. We just need to adjust our perspective.
Also, true darkness is a fixed point of emptiness and the
absence of all light. That has never existed in human form.
We are Everything the Light Touches, including our dark
and ugly voids. So yes, this book will light the way, but
also like the backdrop of midnight's skin, darkness traces
my truth and is the best part of finding that my depth allows
the stars to shine.

Copyright © 2021 Joyce W.

First Publication Date: May 2021
Self-Published: Amazon/Kindle Create
Social Media: Instagram @joyceWords_23

I do not wish to write prose,
I want to live in it.

-JoyceWords

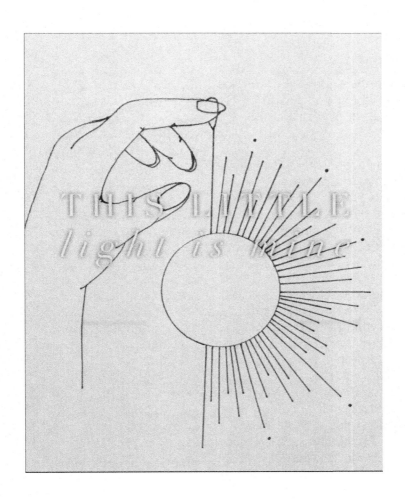

Elizabeth Hernandez did illustration

Contents

Everything the Light Touches

Luminous prisms of color
Made from an artist who only had us in mind
Photons revel in the sunlight.
So, we can see the stars shine.

Oceans.
Blue because the heat and sun drive the currents.
Pulsing softly to refract the tides
Dancing to a frequency divine.

Not all light is visible.

The deeper you go, the more it diminishes.
So, I fall in love, *every time*
With higher kinetic energy;
A God who made my eyes so I could see the serendipity of particles
in a stranger's eyes or the emerald glow of a city against the coves.
A God whose love was so red and so deep, it spilled across the hills and valley.
So, I could feel the tranquility as the colors absorb in the sky.

illustration by JustArtNina

Carl Jung states, "one does not become enlightened by imagining figures of light, but by making the darkness conscious."

Everything You Asked for God is

The first shutter of light in my slowly opening eyes
The first thing I am seeking when my heart is open is the arms of a Persian set sky. He is the sweet whistle tones in birds' breast and the calmness that navigates their wings. He is my chocolates, tissues, and warmth when I am lonely. He is my second chance when I have made a thousand mistakes. God is the flickering embers that kindle in a person's smile. God is the assurance that someone sees you and cares in a world that feels disconnected. He is a text when you desperately need someone to say,

"Are you okay?"

He is the harness that holds you when you are at the end of yourself. God is the healing after pain and the promise that you can hold on to. He will not let you die. He is the unexplainable, the victory, the magic, and the struggles you have overcome. He is the best part of your past.
God is our father, an understanding parent figure that will never bring you shame,

Disappointment, or tell you that you need to change.
God is my break from depression,
as I break from my suppression.
God is the warm rays of light that break behind a storm.
Though the light may seem, little serenity does reside behind the fleece of his heart.

Thank you, God!

Prayer of An Artist

Layer by layer, build me up.
Graph me with the moon of spring.
Diffuse daylight onto my brokenness
until my body vessels summer's light.
I want everyone to see my mosaics of dreams.
Let me create beauty like you created eternity.
May my gifts reflect hope
and the lovely aesthetics
that you have woven into me.
Use your brush to give me purpose,
that way; everyone will get to see
That not everything dark is ugly.

llustration by: DODOMO

Stop It

We have become such a miniature version of ourselves
That we have accepted relationships built out of and consist
of nothing. We are okay with the idea of mutual destruction
because the benefits outweigh the outcome.
Two people who lack love will never find it.
We destroy ourselves by being tethered to their will.
Nukes in our hearts and blocks tied to our ankles.
Somehow drowning in each other is considered passion.
Although you know how to swim
Stop normalizing these Romeo and Juliet types of
relationships.
Stop normalizing shitty friends!
Stop accepting a love that is less than!
Stop It!
Be lonely.
Save you.

It's A God Thing.

I asked for peace,
and He gave me words to prosper.
I craved love, and He said I would be your father.
When people depleted, needed, and receded,
He shaped my pain, and now I never falter.
Sometimes, his mercy is too grand
so, I turn away and ask for a doctor.
If only I could comprehend that in his hands
Mountains move, and life expands.
Then nothing would be a limit.
You can't skim it, don't trim it, live it!
I'm lyrically tuned,
because under his gospel
I bloom.
He gave me peace to part my waters,
He gave me freedom like it's a charter,
He gave me peace to part my waters,
He gave me the strength to overcome,
Alpha and Omega, Yahweh, Emmanuel,
My begging and my end,
my purpose and my grace,
My love-centered,
my spot in the race.

Who I Was Before God Gave me purpose

Abominable shrapnel,
Envy growing from the grotto
pungent lacuna,
Dust of my bones.
Oh, how your lips did turn me
meaningless existence into pleasure.
Death could not touch your vibrant eruptions.
Now, I compose songs to write on paper.
You changed my wayward nature,
from dead weeds
to growing gardens.

Believe in Something.

To survive this life, we must believe in something higher than ourselves. Look at the planets we cannot touch, the sea depths we cannot dive to, the ideas that we cannot grasp, and the time we cannot control. Now believe that there is a power higher than us, a force of balance, justice, and love that constantly protects you. An artist, a God, a deity, call it what you may, but believe it! An idea is a form of peace and a tool for mental strength in a world that, at times, will not make sense. If you believe in something other than Humanity anchors you and gives you a place to put your pain, hurt, and inability to understand why things are. Believe that what you cannot change is not your burden to carry alone, but a divine power supports you, sturdies you, comforts you, and loves you.
Believe in something, or everything will hurt you.

Life Is Hard

Retrograde walks as we skate past our youth
on the precipice of free but suspended
in dark waters of fear.
The more you reach,
the harder it seems
Life is an eternity of treading water,
so, close your eyes and float.
The sun shall dazzle upon your face, a
crystal reflection of earthly foreplay.
When it is hard, steady your heart in
the sands of serenity, and life will drift
you to serendipity.
Never lose your light,
it will revive you.

What If?

And what if all the strange
things about you
were perfect?
Your weird quirks,
the way you laugh at your jokes,
Talk too loudly and interrupt yourself.
The way you dance when you are all alone,
or sing at the top of your lungs,
or cry when things frustrate you.
The sky looks different every day.
Get lost in the light,
the idea of the imperfect is
perfect for you.

Notes from a sinner, trying to understanding God:

I understand what sin means.

It is not just making a bad decision or understanding the difference between right and wrong. Sin seeps into our quality of life, like air pollution. It is like a deep tar that permeates through the fabric of light, spilling into our lungs.

Close your eyes and envision a world covered in dense smoke clouds. See the silhouette of darkness against every building, as if midnight has fallen onto the once shining city. Everything is dark, but not a visual, more of a texture. It is thick and suffocating like bellowing funnels of soot. Yet, people are tiptoeing like ants through this inexhaustible contamination, going about freely practicing their mundane rituals.

Never feeling how cold and distant the world is

If you look closely, you can see the starved depravity in their hollow eyes as they itch and fester in their dingy grotesque environment. Still, they call it home. Sin is a state of being, we live in it, and that will not change. Yet, it is our responsibility to try. God's love and blood are the only antidotes to this condition, but in return, he wants us to fight the good fight, to show him love, loyalty, and that we are worth his sacrifice. Sin has tentacles, and it latches onto your soul, stealing what God has endowed to you. (Your state of purity that is bound to your rose gold vines.)

Do you ever wonder why no one sins once?

For example, if you lust, you have probably had a progression of steady thoughts that led to that moment of desire. If you drink, it is not just one sip, and if you lie, you are a liar, etc. I think you get it. Sin is a deep recurrence, with heavy chains, meant to control you. I am not saying this to scare you into being a perfect Christian because, quite frankly, that is impossible. I do not believe that we will ever be sinless if we abide on this earth. Remember, it is a condition that God must come and remove us from. (Hence the reason why God is coming back to get us, to pull us and take us to the new Jerusalem) it is the placement that is imperative to note.

Understanding sin helps me know that God is not just an annoying parent telling you what to do. He is a powerful, omnipotent force, a deity of purity, fighting more extraordinary powers than we could ever imagine, and for that, I owe him my life. So, I do not promise to be perfect, and I promise to be aware that his grace and mercy deliver me from the trenches of our condition. I promise to wipe the soot from my eyes enough to look up at the sky and give him praise for his light in our blindness. I promise to live the best I can even with my condition because without him, and we are ill, fractures of walking tempers, dust in the wind, nothing.

Sin shows me that the antidote is God's love.

Magnets

I ran into this stranger, and immediately I wanted to know them. Perhaps it was the quietness that settled in their eyes like the dark husk beneath the moon or the allure of night. Yet, they felt oddly familiar and safe.

As time went on, I found myself frustrated because I would often run into them.

But they would never allow me to know them.

Instead, a solid wall would always greet me.

They held me at a distance in a space where I could reach but never grasped how badly I needed them to need me.

So, one day I spewed out my frustrations.

I screamed, "why don't you love me?"

I have shown you kindness,

Attention,

Patience,

And everything you asked for.

I chase you because that is what love is.

I think about how you feel, so I consider all the possibilities of what makes you happy.

I am thoughtful.

Then the stranger picked up a mirror, and I realized all along I was upset at myself.

Parts of me were dead, and in that death, I searched for life amongst coffins and broken flower pots. I searched the empty peaks and valleys. I looked for life like it was the last drop of water.

Only to find that life had left me…

Projected into the past, I saw the little girl who still needed me, to be brave, to rise out of the debris, and to carry her thudding heart softly. I was attracted to barren trees and empty shells because we often follow what we have seen. We often embody what we lack or what we need,
I found that my deficiencies drew forth a giant hole.

Magnets

This is for you.

I know what it feels like to have the weight
of the world on your shoulders,
and one more feather is what breaks you.

I know how the darkness surrounds you, so you feel like
there isn't any light.
I understand what it feels like to be trapped in your mind.

You aren't the events that break you.
You aren't the events that break you.
You aren't the hate that hates you.

I get what nothing feels like,
empty tiredness, a sore heart,
and a rattling mind.

You have felt like this forever.
So, you've given up believing that
you can shift the tides.

You aren't alone.

Don't you see the angels around you?
The people who love you
Strong arms like wings to carry you an extra mile.
Like soldiers, they surround you, and No one will hurt you;
nothing can take you.

I know what sadness feels like.
It can be like a penny floating to the bottom of the ocean,
an infinity of darkness, drowning in its depth.
Sometimes sadness is a smile, a face you have worn
without stitches.

Say it with me.
You will get through this
I know because,
I am you.

If you stay

The pain won't.
Islands will shape wherever your feet burrow.
Waves will gather your freedom.
Love will cradle the fragments, the jaded pieces, and
 the cosmic dust underneath your eyes.
If you stay,
your love will be the light that makes the stars jealous.
If you wait, you will be the rhythmic muse of someone's
unfinished masterpiece.
The steel fist that oscillates between the husk of daybreak
and what you have overcome.
Your essence will be phosphorescent crystals of laughter
and pulsing yellows in a wildfire of luminescent ecstasy.
If you stay,
you will be STRONG.

It is Okay Not to Be Perfect

If you had trouble cleaning yourself up today
It is perfectly fine
If you have not showered, let my encouragement be like
cool refreshing rain in a foreign tropic summer.
You are the center of paradise, even when you are tired.
You are my rosemary mint, and no state of mind, no
tattered soil clothes, or lack of personal hygiene can take
away your value or beauty.
I remember who you used to be.
I still see your inner child.
Reach out your hand, and I will pull you from the depths of
your sorrow.
I will never judge you for having this moment.
There is no such thing as a fault when you break.
Think of gardens,
for beautiful things to eventually grow,
seeds submerge in darkness (soil) until they grow roots.
Then the pain of beauty begins as they sprout, penetrating
through the surface, reaching for the sun.
Facing every element, they must learn to withstand
until their stems and roots are stronger.
They flourish.
So, will you.

Everything You Need

The motion of the Stars
The earth spins in circles,
not the stars.
They dance in a celestial sphere
a constellation.
Little star,
You must have the courage to shine.
The sky needs you.
Don't doubt what you can and can't do,
just discover the scope of your luminous brilliance.

It breaks my heart to think most of us are living dimly,
Because of fear.
Because of people
Because of a past, that feels permanent.
The earth (life) spins (moves) in circles,
Not the stars (you).

How does a star stay in place?
It is held together by its gravity.
You are everything
you need.

A Reminder of Who You Are

I want you to know that
you capture the quality of light.
It is the way you trace the movement of colors,
Poppy seeds, clay reds, and cadmium yellows,
Deepening to the touch of your tone.
I want you to know
that your smile gives us space to aspire, like the
strokes and impressions on a colorless canvas.
You are the beautiful things,
only the eyes can translate to the heart.
Even when you shutter into dark things,
Even when you change.
You emerge as someone greater.
God makes no mistakes.
I want you to know,
You are a radiant soul!
A composition of variegated timbres
siphoned by envious elements and oils.
Without you,
Life would not mean.

I want you to know you are special

We Matter

We are the same narrative,
although our strings may be different.
We align at the center of our soul.
I am not one.
I am part of my collective,
like flowers teeming and abundant,
understories of the forest.
I reach for validation, a torch of divinity.
A variety of bright, explosive colors,
an orchestra of Poppies.
Don't step on us.
We matter!

Cycles

We are born kicking and
screaming, so we awaken to the light.
Fighting for the air we breathe in, conquering our fright.
Blood against our bones, envy in our sight.
There my garden grows,
From the ruptures in my soul.
I hope, like the cycles, we decompose.
It is time to let the old me go.

Advice Because it Only Gets Easier

Stop sharing your stories
with people who don't like to read,
and bend the tip of pages in books.
They don't deserve to be a part of
your best chapter.
Some of us spend our whole life waiting
for the right tools and conditions.
We've got to understand that we can move
mountains with just our bare hands.
There will never be a perfect time
Do it now!

Beauty.

If they can't breathe life into you
Then they don't have the power to break you.
You were made in the image of love
No one else looks like you.
Roses on the inside,
pick YOU

illustration by: StockLeb

Being Present- Note to Self

Wake Up.
Prepare to see the parts that are decrepit,
Worn out, used, and in a state of utter despair,
And know that love can reawaken in the ruins of
things that have slipped away
Because sometimes that what's
showing up means.

I AM HEALING

Is that okay?
My essence is frayed from being everyone's napkin
I'm happy you cleaned up nicely
Can I be tired?
Can I rest behind the facade of peaceful blue?
Floating softly, a retinue of security.
I have traveled to the depths of love for you,
Now I have sore soul aches.
I am empty, but you never notice; you just hate that I've
changed.
I've been pushed to the brink of sane
I give myself permission to breathe, to need,
and understand that kindness has the gentlest hands.
If I lose all my marbles, it's okay
 because that means I lose all my hurt too.
I am healing; I will renew.

You Deserve This

I hope everyone sees your fulgent colors,
Your sapphires, the jaded hues, and violet streaks
I pray you to finish the puzzle,
I know you have spent your whole life waiting for the last
piece. You deserve the ebullience echoes of laughter as
your heartbeats.
You deserve the sweet smooth embrace of security that
mimics a rasp in a singer's rifting key.
You deserve a good meal at the dinner table
because you have always given so much more than what
they need. You deserve a plethora of wondering things
because I know how hard it can be to shape character
around dull things.
You deserve to know that your pain is not your defeat
because light breaks through the tiniest of fractures.
You will win, not a race, but a life of rich peace.

I Cherish You

Your kindness is a fragrance, carried
like pollen on the tiny legs of Honeybees.
Your spirit is lighter than frolicking butterflies,
drifting breathlessly in a lemon aura.
Little soul kites fanned across the great blue.
You are fissions of strength,
fastened in gentle pulsing lights.
Don't forget you are the force of currents,
even when you cry.
You imbue with lavender buds of humanity.
An Avant-Garde composer, "eutony" flowing in my rhyme
Smoking sputters of eternal change, beauty's reflection.
Don't let time forget you, and do not drown in its past.
Never forget,
You are everything the light touches.

Behind the Light

What I want people to see the most is not the sun in my
eyes, but how people and experience shape how I play with
light. If I hold it long enough, it feels like my focal point.
It's not always about being strong or beautiful; some days,
it's about being brave enough.
To stand up to me. Brave enough to put the pain behind me
and not live in the crevices of hate. Sometimes it gets dark
and grainy because so many places feel empty and leave
me wondering why I placed my heart there?
But I know we are everything the light touches,
which means it is easy to take our own for granted.
We will always reflect hope and beauty.

BE CRAZY!

Don't hold back,
Roll on the floor
Scream until your voice is the only
the thing that matters
Undo these chains!
Raise your hands,
marshal the madness.
Leap across the shadows,
Shake out your demons.
Let your body flow,
Dance in Bourbon,
play in hurricanes.

Maybe you must be a little crazy
To survive this life.
Because nothing makes sense

KEEP GOING

If you ever feel like you started late
or that your dreams are always delayed.
No one ever feels time; it is about direction, not speed.
Time moves in a state of an exquisite order.
And you are the energy in the center,
bursting like techno colors.
So, don't make space for granted; fill it with laughter, fill it
with memories,
I love all the beautiful seconds in between,
gather the chaos, and let it teach you things.
Be the entropy on a continuous fabric of silver linings.
Here is a paradox,
time will have its time.
You will have your time,
Keep pushing forward.

It is Perfectly Acceptable to feel like Shit.

You have been rubbed together like brass and gold,
Scathed against hurtful words like jagged stones.
Your lungs have carried the ocean,
so you are heaving up foam.
Goals feel like drowning, legs made of stone.
Body aches like ceaseless tremors because
everyone who said they would never leave,
did.
You may be feeling like darkness is an old soul,
making plans
for you to come home.
Your body feels like lightning,
 blue currents in electrical poles,
you are overcharged but afraid and alone.
When you feel like this,
Rest.

Shower of Comets

Some of us are comets.
Burning ice
Leaving traces of who we are
across a seamless line.
Don't hold back
as you circle the sun.
You precious being of celestial growth!
Know that people look up to you on nights.
Wondering why they can't touch
your glowing aurora.

It may feel like falling, but gravity,
only wishes to be closer to you.
You shape the paths of the planets,
Sometimes you lead with feelings,
exuberant passions that shower
the sky.

Understand that some people will be
afraid to love you.

Because you are a force of projected brilliance,
Heading for a world that is too simple.
Even when you collide,
 boundless, and withering,
bursting at the speed of light,
your halo still
shines bright.

Draw Your Feelings (Activity)

We Are Who We Are

You trace the
grooves,
never wondering where they lead.
Stars searching,
we only exist in relation to someone else.

Sensitive to the touch of our nuance,
stuck in a nursery of solipsism
because the exploration of self is all we have.
Rocks in our pockets distressed like our denim.
Walking heavy

We are an orchestra of fluidity without a purpose.
Chaos and angst lost in composure.
Charred tints.
The antithesis between love and rationality
Strawberry stains on Bomber Jackets.
Smoke clouds in my lungs, wheezing for love.

You kiss to find yourself,
I kiss so that other people know me.
Eyes eclipse
So, we never lose the feeling
Never lose feeling
Never lose feel

Did we make art yet?

Meditate.

Let your breath catch the lightness of dandelion spurs,
as they worship the sun
Their hearts are attracted to the warmest places.
Pretend your shoulders are tides rowing back and forth.
Push your worries to the back of tomorrow, bring the
vibrant depth
of love closer to you!
Now let freedom be your blood,
trace it like rivers running
Unequivocally calm,
 breathe
Luminescent streaks, shimmering pools.
Go deep into the Morando sunset.
Escape and find your strength.
You are the flames of poetry,
set the lonely parts of you on fire.
Let your pain drip, like an Italian summer.
Leave the fragments of yourself in every tree
as you listen to all the beautiful promises
your body sings.
Tomorrow will be better; tomorrow will be better.
You are better!

She turned and said,

I can't be small today.
Magnificent souls don't
fit into tiny structures.
They build worlds.

HOPE

Hope is the honey that suckles on your breath, making
every word sweet.
Hope is a splinter that you feel but never seem to see.
Hope is the sea you chart while the tides rise in your eyes
 and crash against your heart.
Hope is the strength you have when nothing is left.
Hope is the silence that spills out of the fountains as you
throw
away from your wishes.
When the stars forget that they must stand out from the sky
to shine
Only then will you understand
That you have always been hope

You Are Not

We will at times be separated,
dappled with opaque feelings and atrophied.
In these moments, remember that not everything
broken or bent signifies
You are not your depression.
You are not the dark fractures that pass through your
empty.
You are not the negative voice you hear deep inside.
You are just a moment, a dispersion of light.
It's okay to be experimental and pure.
Race you to the silver line!

Osmosis

Then she gathered up all her wreckage
knowing that she deserved more than
thoughts that weighed like ashes
Knowing that she needed
more than coruscating promises
from barren palms.
Tired of always falling,
and coming out the other side
without values or boundaries.
For the first time,
 in a while
She wanted to protect her stunning
sphere.
The lambent
Immeasurable, extraordinary,
crystal of her soul.
So, she took her lows and went far.
She was building beauty.

Dark Purple

You are easy to love.
You escape the narrative of beauty,
as language is selfish and keeps all the ways it
wants to ravish you, lost.
So, know that even when their mute,
they are jealous.
I see how delicate,
 you tremble in one's mind.
Fluid, in all the depths you trace,
so, people never forget the impression
 of your warmth.
God gave some of your
angelic light to the moon.
So, we could see past our darkness.

Euphemism

The fine morning sun extends across the sky
to watch you,
distilled, and fearless.
Airy, as you dream.
Jealous because you are fearless.
How it wishes, it could glow like you.
Honey.

illustration by: ArtistMiki

Good is Coming!

I feel a storm stirring in my chest,
this time life will be different.
Spiral fumes of ecstatic feelings,
as I move toward MY great.
Take me as I am, a delicate flower.
Freedom like the
birds who slow dance in
the humming monologues
of the golden sun.
I dance for hope.
Sleeping in sunflower beds, a litany of prayers
In the streams of change
I feel a storm stirring in my chest
Praise on the inside, so good things are coming!

Phenomenal Woman

This happiness is no longer a mask,
I have permitted myself to live.
I had tasted culture through travel and the depth
of making do when I had nothing.
I have beat the statics, I have recalculated the algorithm,
I have defined my physics by becoming the chasm,
and I have broken the system.
These chains cannot hold me!
I have risen, not once, but every day and I fought the good
fight.
While looking beautiful and exquisite
My ego is humbled, and I am grateful for every.
Little thing. I have gotten in the ring with my fears and
played with
the nature of butterflies and bees.
I have sat patiently in my cage, painting my dreams.
I have seen what my bravery can be watching it change the
times,
from a girl's heart to a big screen, from a place of multi-
colors to rich ebony.
I have learned to accept every version of me.
I have been *Thoreau* and *Wilde* when it comes to studying
the nature of love.

Ask me why I am a Phenomenal Woman?
Ask me.
And I will scream from the mountain's top,
Because "I am Happy!"

Now is Your Time.

Gather up your youth; now is the time you rise.
You were made to move, to be as fluid as the
sprinting air that flumes through your heavy thoughts.
Be electric-like fires in the depths of your vivid soul
Pour the ocean until you discover what is underneath its
blue, make love to the depth of your passions because self-
love is an art!
Provoke beauty until it follows with envy and wears it like
a shimmering. Blood blush. Run till the lines disappear, and
heaviness eclipses into
fluorescent showers of Rubies.
Be strong enough to shatter your past.
Become one with this life because happiness
cannot be found insensibility but in the tremors of your
pain, and differences.
Have faith, and believe
Now is the time to rise!

How Do I Change?

Bring flowers, wear black,
and fall into a metaphorical coffin.
Appreciate the strength of the old ways,
and be prepared for the delight of change.
Let your rebirth be without fear or criticism.
Admire the fractures because that's where light grows.
Change one habit at a time,
 fail and get back up.
Laugh, love, and enjoy the shimmering sunrise as you
create new islands.
Like magnetism,
 know that good things are coming towards you.
You are your law of motion.
As long as you try, energy will flow into you.
Pray, focus, be kind,
 and repeat, and repeat, and repeat.

"Now I got you in my space I won't let go of you"- Latch
by Disclosure (Song quote)

It's Okay to Love,

I can't give you my heart,
It's all that's left of me.
It's bruised, and tender, and even
the slightest advance
abuses me.
I am a bear in a cave, looking for warmth,
But if you get too close
Still, I am seventy percent honey.
You might catch a splinter
when I feel brave enough to let you see.
I think I want love desperately,
But I accept what was given to me.
Day by day, I teach myself that it is okay to love.
The first step never starts with people, but with myself.
It's okay, I promise.

Filters

Instagram, Tik Tok, and Snapchat,
Changed how I saw myself
A false perception of real reality.
I realized that my anxiety and
depression provided a filter as well,
one in which beauty is skewed.
Depression darkens the day, and fear
takes away the focus, in a blur of feelings.
Yet the truth is you are enough.
You are still the most beautiful sonnet
God has ever written
And you are worth so much more than
your circumstances, and pain.
You are the rising sun!

I am working hard to take off the filters.

How People See You

You do not tiptoe around beauty
But immerse in its sober light,
compelling us all to be our best.
Your touch dances like smoke,
so soft that hate will never understand you.
You walk around like midnight,
lost in a trance of self-depreciation,
But darling, you embody dawn in your heart.
Rising spurs of synthesis dipped in Honey Red.
Wings do extend to bathe in your afterglow,
to know you, to have the privilege
of being tethered to the very space, you exist.
People see your lovely; they see your kindness,
they see your fluent beauty even if you cannot see it
yourself.

Dedicated to my Sunbeam Family

You Cacophony

Roar like rapid rivers crashing against the mountains,
Trample through your thickets of hardship with loud
snares.
Don't ever die quietly!
Be a rebel of thunder; push the air of change around you.
You must be loud because sometimes your perfect reticent
reflection traps everything good inside.
reflection traps everything good inside
Scream like there is no feeling in a pit of fire!
Rise until the sky falls, and then you can experience it.
What it means to walk on water

I've Been in Love Lately

We describe love as something fast.
But love thoughtfully ponders on every side of our form, so
That it never misses a glimpse of beauty.
I think love is slow, like the dazzling arches of the day
breaking across a landscape or a tractor plowing its delicate
fingers against her sooty soil, a slow coax to flourish. It
must be a deep impression, a delicate fleur.

I know love is God.

His love is the same as building a home,
the same skills, and concrete foundations.
Therefore, I say love is slow.
Because we still abide in his home.
The one he created when nothing could be turned to light
Yes, feelings are captivating, as the mist silk threads of dew
showers the leaves in the morning or the curious clouds that
inch across the sky.

Love means nothing without time because time is salvation
working retrospectively to give us opportunities to change
and define.

God's love never ceases.

If God loved us once, would it mean much?
Would it be considered grace?
Yet he wants us infinitely. He never crumbled the stars, the
moon, and the air around us despite our sinful natures. I am
here because his love never started over or gave up on his
creation.

He tells us that he is jealous of all the places you put him next to, all the focus and energy you left waiting for someone else to pay attention to. Like playing chess, you make your moves, but all he wants is to have you.
God is indeed a romantic because his feelings can be said in one line. "You are my comma; I'll wait for you."

Love is slow

Jeremiah 31:3 The Lord appeared to him from far away. I have loved you with an everlasting love; therefore, I have continued my faithfulness to you.

I have been in love lately.

Dear_____
_____ (INSERT NAME)

You do not deserve me.

Agape

Love, you put the lavender sun behind the set and called it
to rain. You stole the yellow lines from the road, endless
aches. We kissed the modern soul and spat the healing.
We fell into the cold, like a London love.
You are the reason I shelved while kneeling.
We loved until we became ghosts behind the clouds.
Howling like death, we faired down
We ground our fingers into the cords, collecting the blues.
Our love was like shadows settled in the planes,
Agape.

I Have One Question?

If you are the type of person
who notices the beauty of morning's light, loves to take
long walks, and listens to the earth breathe.
If you are the type of person who finds every shade of
human unique and wonderful,
Loves to accessorize their outfits,
And enjoys a broad spectrum of music,
collects aesthetically pleasing pens and is drawn
too bright or rich colors.
Then you know the value of beauty.
I have one question.
Why haven't you picked?
You?

Don't You Dare Give Up!

I know your heart is full.
Eager to have every dream, wanting to change.
I know it is bigger than you,
and that is why you can't give up.

Finding Peace in the Quiet

Most nights, I am alone,
breath suspended in the sighs of
my loud fan and empty basin of thoughts.
It took me a while to find peace because
love was never shown as a moment or pause.
It was never silent and still like the rocking waves
between the horizon and offshore.
Like currents in a wild storm,
I was always reaching
for stability and acceptance on sinking islands.
To the point of exhaust, but
even fires burn out.
Because I born in the chaos, I couldn't appreciate the still,
Like bobbing boats tinkering on the blue.

Now, most nights, I am content,
Enjoying the gentleness of rain, tapping against my
window. The chamomile thud of my heart, a soothing
rhythm of a conductor's baton,
In a symphony of lights
My whizzing fan, twirling in the dust of milky blue décor,
And a dalliance of self and comfort.
I am reserved like the moon,
Centered and settled
in my opulent pastiche, waiting for the night to
carry on its magic,
knowing that I am okay.

When you are alone write down the thoughts that come to mind, use them to create a poem. (Activity)*

Example:
Your thoughts
I am hungry, I need to leave, nice red boots, the sky is cloudy, and I miss my bed.

Your poem

Red boots in a cloudy sky,
Following my thoughts with hunger.
I miss my bed.

I Had to Let you Go

Scathed, you took all my skin,
Dragging me along, holding me at the
end of your sanity.
Bruises, I thought it was real,
so I refused to see how much it was hurting me.
I left, so you could find your own
villain and not put it all on me.
I left because gold only sinks in water.

Fear Not

I had to learn.
Not to be afraid of me.
I knew that I carried the
 power of oceans in my palms.
I could make everything move except myself.
I was taught to love everyone except me,
To help, grow, and support you
Before everything,
So, doing something for myself,
It was a cruel punishment

We sink so softly,

Some of us fall in love with
pain, so we eagerly await its deepening touch.
Despair can be comely; it floats like morning dew,
Drinking from the cusp of all we envision.
It rocks us gently until we are not bothered by the feeling
of being numb. It keeps us warm on lonely nights, a deep
aching. That we invite in. Like winter's sleepy shadows, it
nestles in, watching us drink to forget, hazy and lifeless.
We sink so softly into this space,
that we often mistake it
as home.

Running from It All

The open street hummed as her breath beat against the pavement. Soft lights twinkled behind the city mountain, watching the world through a telescope of stars. She was running to surrender, like a trajectory force, flung by her ideations. Sometimes this life made her feel like an unrequited stranger or a traveler who could never find a rest stop. Constantly tired but pushing forward. She was running so she wouldn't fall apart because moving reminded her that she was in motion. She was running through a tunnel of light, a blur of pixelated moments, like water spilled on ink; she was leaving the dark pigments behind. People said she moved too fast, but she searched for a temple and searched past the short pieces of her soul for something real. Sweat streamed down her face forming holy rivers. She would keep running because if she stopped, then she would remember the pain she left behind.

What are you running from?
*(Writing Prompt)

I am running from,_____

_

You were.

God is!
Everything changed.
I did not believe in miracles
until my life became one.

Don't Grow Up

Chart the Sapphire seas
because you know there is a treasure. (self-worth)
Leap and bound, in make-believe places, fearless
because falling just gives you practice for your wings.
Catch fireflies, play with worms and stain
all your clothes in woodsy forest fantasies. (freedom)
Express emotions without shame because your innocence
provokes a mural of feelings. (expression)
Take naps, spit out your peas because quite frankly
they are repulsive! (reject)
Don't grow up,
because society says it's not acceptable
to love and be who you are.
Just stay a child forever.

Fire Starter

Let go of your anger; although warranted, it will burn
through acres and acres of your beautiful.
It will destroy all this is kind within you and steal your
youth.
People mostly describe anger as a fire, but it is also a thread
with multiple points of origin. It starts simple, but over time
it becomes complicated. Then one day, you find that this
unbreakable, tangled, destructive knot is you.

Are you angry?

I Come First.

Don't put people in a position to have to choose
between you and what they desire.
Let them show you that their position and desire is you

Boundaries

When a storm comes, barriers are built to protect the homes around the ocean.
Our space and peace should be the same because floods bring ruins, broken pieces,
shards, debris, and fragments of other people's baggage and waste toward us.
You do not deserve to drown in another people's mess.

You can do this.

You can be alone.
I'm sorry that your mind has played tricks on you
Like shadows against the wall, only showing you
 the darkening depths of your loneliness.
Now it is your time to turn on the light.
Paint a tapestry of colors on the voids of sadness, use
the black to deepen the purples hues, and wine reds.
Trace the moonlight and create in the ebony still.
Laugh until humor reshapes the pain and cast the demons
into the dark.
Dance, play, explore, travel, make life jealous of how brave
you are!
You are everything the light touches.

Change Is Scary

I don't like change.
I don't like to change my favorite flavor of ice cream,
Or my morning routine, not to mention the chaotic system I call cleaning.
I don't do well with people who start sentences with, "Let's try something different."
Because change is what took my grandmother, one day, she just wasn't here
Change is what makes the person who swears they love you the most and break their promise of forever.
Change is what makes friends a moment in our story.
But change also helps push hurt along because it often likes to sit with leisure, making itself comfortable on the big red plush of our hearts.
The change also turns the night today and dark to light.
Change gives us numerous opportunities to grow and be loved a thousand times.
It fills the hollow with laughter and protects us from getting stuck, like a broken recorder on one thought.
Change gives us beauty because it is beautiful how far we have come.
Change gives us healing when we are sick and tired of it all.
I would hate to be just one thing in this miraculous part of life.
So yes, I still do not like change,

But you could say my mind is changing

MY SUPPORT

Me: What if I lose my mind?
Friend: If you lose all your marbles,
 I'll pick them up for you.

-Thank you, God, for my good friends
Dedicated to O

Kind Words

"You are enough.

You are enough.

Nothing about you needs to be changed.

You are enough.

Now fill the empty spaces with love and self-acceptance."

Write A List of Things You Love About Yourself.

1.
2.
3.
4.
5.
6.
7.
8.
9.
10.
11.
12.
13.
14.
15.

Self-Love is Freedom.

She created her eurhythmics,
flowing so freely in her eternal profoundness.
Wherever she went, love followed, never a chase,
but a place in a higher design.
Her crown was made of crystals, and fluorescent shapes
as she learned how to love her inner child.
No one can define
No one can define
No one can define
How lovely she would be.
A sparkling pulse of phenomenal energy!
She created her movement,
By becoming her magic,
Pretty Little Alchemist.

It's Not Your Storm

A tiny figure stood at the shoreline,
in the middle of an October storm.
The wind howled with anger dragging its
turbulent and cruel wrath against the sea.
The waves screamed, rising like towers threatening
to bruise the clouds, until they bled darkness, and
drowned in the gloomy day's abyss.
The sea roared, taunting the figure on the shore,

"I dare you to fight me!"

The figure of the shore pondered for a moment
 as the sea ravaged everything with its fist.
Turning beauty into dust, crumbling dreams, and stomping
on hope.

Yet they waited patiently, watching the destruction and
chaos expand,
and the wind created funnels of water, forming hurricanes.
The figure also noticed a slither of light breaking
just behind the caliginous dismal sky.

Finally, they decided to respond,

"No, I won't fight you, but I'll wait until you get tired."

*Sometimes, it is not your battle; it's not your depression
or responsibility to fight against the storm that threatens
you.
Love yourself enough to wait it out, and dawn is just
around the corner.

What to say to people who hurt you?

I owe you a thank you.
Thank you for teaching me what hurts,
Because now I know what heals.

Zero Plus Zero is Still Zero

You can't care for people more
 than they do, and you can't love yourself
 more than what is reflected in your present truth.
It's nice to be imaginative, but even better to be real.
Otherwise, it is just an empty grave of dreams.
Zero Plus Zero is Still Zero,
and One plus Zero is still One.

Focus

Standing in the center of it all
You feel everything, even the thinnest traces of worry.
You see the beauty of life, but even the popping colors
present overstimulation.
You care for people who take every limb and breath away
from you.
Unraveling your lifeline
The energy you give is the energy you lose.
Moments flurry past you like people in a museum.
You sit quietly watching them, and time watches you.
Art in motion, except you are the statue.
Focus.
Turn down the dial with deep breaths, collect the essence of
you.
Like a telescope, adjust your lens, change the perspective.
And close the distance between you and what you desire.
Now see all the wonderful things about you, discover the
roads that lead to
the worth inside you.
Focus.
Understand that you never have to chase anything that is
meant for you,
Like a magnet, great things are drawn to you when you
Focus.

Love Letters (Part 1)

I am trying to love you like God,
pouring purpose into you.
In the same way, he filled the black olive soot with
tiny traces of starlight to picture the sky.
He made matter, and now everything empty brims
with traces of milky particles.

I am trying to teach you to wait for all the good
things to come.
Sometimes you worry about your place in life,
but know that God is the point above the sky,
directly below an observer.
I love you like Joseph's dreams, trickling showers
 of God's impression over your life.

I love you like the beauty that ran through Esther,
enough to move the space between hate and people.
I want to love you like a job, and one day you will trust me,
knowing that no tribulation or agony
will break the love between us.

You will endure.

I am trying to love you like God,
 so that his constellation of love refracts into
the unsettled parts of your body.
I am trying to love you like God.
Because he uses stars to guide his people

Love Letter Prompt

Now write your own.

Dear, _____You are the reason I_____

Love Letters (Part 2)

Loving me is winter's wet dream.
I am the warmest parts of a kindling fire, cascading across
dreary cold nights.
Loving me is an eternal delight, branded in arcadian
dreams.
Exquisite goddess that I am!
When I love, my delicate nature is a refuge
enveloped in a fresh blanket of snow.
Defined to catch all your satin desires
When I shiver, each ice kissed breath descends gently
to awaken
the most beautiful.
You will never meet another me!

How We Can Choose to See the Hard Moments

Maybe we should see hard moments like lightning,
Black and white flashes against a graphite sheet.
Electrical currents of heat, incandescent tempers
Tears transverse across the city, running down the form.
Just for a brief pause, be caught in the furry
of feeling.
There are radiant lanterns right behind the fleece of
heavy clouds,
Light always shadows the shade,
waiting for the aching dark realm to
Be peaceful again.

I Am Not A Tool Box

Some people don't like you
Because you give less than you use to,
and they can no longer use you.
You didn't lose anything but a leech.

Who Am I?

I am echoes of disparity sheathed in poverty.
I am my ancestor's stories, deep and rich like fangs.
I am the all the things people said, "I couldn't be,"
I am the color you judged so blindly before the person.
I am the words of hate you spewed, black tar running
from your ill-fated lips.
But MOSTLY
I am a divinity of light, the blood of the body, love of light.
God's favorite instrument, an ever-constant flux of holy
beauty! I am the day that breaks the river, a graceful nuance
of consciousness.
I am an ultra-light beam; colors dance in waves as love
ripples through me.
I am the third finger when all the rest are tired, a strong
salute to humanity.
I am perfectly and wonderfully made, which is why I am
not ashamed.
I am **EVERYTHING THE LIGHT TOUCHES.**
So, the real question is, "Who are you?"

There is No Shame in Our Ecosystem

I know it is hard to even when you are trying.
Not even the waves can push themselves, the light can't be produced
without energy, and the moon uses the world like stilts to rise. Sometimes we feel like we must carry everything on our shoulders, but even gravity needs to keep us from falling. Everything in this world needs something or someone to carry them.
Don't be afraid to ask for help.
I am here to support you.

National Suicide Hotline 1(800)-273-8255

AFFIRMATIONS

I am a precious sunbeam,
a radiant source of life and energy.
Everything I touch flourishes, so today
I promise to be
my own garden.

New Discoveries.

Welded-in a storm of lights,
Wings brush against the tavern taps of nights,
dripping Jadeite, wherever you go.
Some may try to break you,
but like fireflies, you emit your source of brightness.
People are deeply intoxicated by your radiance and
sway in your aura.
Admiring the way, you walk in your birthright,
don't sink behind the shadows,
Never knowing that you are bioluminescent!

Content

I have found myself,
Sitting quietly by the river.
Resting peacefully in the folds of glory,
Bathing in a rippling reflection of wholeness.
I exist because
God poured the morning sun
onto a single thought.

Question to consider: Who were we before someone told us what makes us happy?

Life is So Beautiful

We are a collection of choices, dusted off by the silver
threads of the universe.
We will take long walks of ethics, and sometimes we forget
to choose ourselves.
We must relinquish the chains that hold us back and
immerse ourselves in freedom.
Be free from the asphalt that corrodes your mind, don't let
spiteful
words break you.
Healing is a joyful *Hallelujah*!
So, don't fear change, cocoon my little poet, and shed the
old pain.
God's spirit will guide your metamorphosis and synthesize
your zeal,
to change the tides.
One day soon, your wings will impress the sky,
Even in the darkness, your light pierces
Be a butterfly.

Lost in the Depths

Many nights I prayed,
waiting for a shutter of hope.
Couldn't see me, couldn't feel my worth
I fell between the composition of stars, lost in
A spectrum of light.
Bobbing in an astrological storm, tarnished
By the ultra-night
Shattered like a prism,
So, I had to carry and focus my shine.
I realized that I am greater than any
 visible light.
I stopped sleeping in aphotic voids
and created my approach.
Now my life defines,
and I no longer need to hold up
the stratosphere,
Because I am a master of light.
I am the SUN
no matter the mood of the sky!

Phases of the Moon

The sun is the main source of light in this universe
, a bright glow across an infinite scope of darkness.
There is no such thing as moonlight.
We see the side of
the moon that is facing the sun's smile through
each cycle.
The other side is dark.
Although we experience pain, melancholy,
and defeat.
Like the phases of the moon
We are not the darkness that eclipses.
We will orbit,
and touch the light again.

Let that sink in.

Your name is,

I give you a new name.
You are here for a reason.
Surrender to your dancing blood
follow the flow
Tapping feet and an enormous smile.
Love in the torrent, resplendent spirit
flames bespoke to fit your soul.
I give you a new name,
Happy

One Day I Will Be Strong

Black moon with freckles
In a mane of tangerine dust
Vivid canary petals
eclipsed in vibrant greens
Tall stalks of wisdom
Sun soul, how I love your seeds.
Swaying in the arms of a gentle breeze.
You are not delicate but a firm and powerful being.
Do you ever stop reaching for the sun?
I cannot pick you,
I adore your precious ways.
One day I will grow
 sunflowers across
my empty plains.

light[7]

/līt/ verb

- The love we give. (to everyone, especially ourselves)

Synonyms: spirit, portions of divinity, warmth, hope, smile, kindness, courage, etc

.How We Make Light

Move.
Rise like prayers
Amongst the fray of the day
Deep stirs that charge and evoke
the origami kites of your heart.
Bring the sun in until you radiate outwards.
Freedom is a charge,
Forward, steady and strong
 in its triumph.
When it all goes pitch dark,
abysmal and sonder.
You will be the atom
that dances among a sea of bright!
The way you give light is what makes it.

What is It that We Need?

It's not about being happy.
Because even when I'm sad, there is a depth
to that feeling that conjures beauty.
Feelings are fragile, and they never seem to be yours.
Like when I feel all the ways, you love me but don't.
I guess that's called "Chasing my Imagination."

I can't tell you exactly we need, but I know
We should put ourselves first.
Loving life and filling our pockets with experiences
That makes us feel alive and inspired.
I think we were born to be antique collectors, builders, and
farmers of life.

For example, when the sun loves the world,
even softly, we all feel it's a warm embrace
So, you deserve to be the rays that the sun gives us each
morning.
You deserve to flourish.
It starts when we love ourselves,
Nicely.

I want to go to Paris.

Repeat After Me

My soul is irrefutably the center of love.
I keep every exchange, every current of memories like
love letters close to the aching, lonely parts.
I reserve myself for those who seek not to destroy beautiful
things.
In my hiding is a lovely, budding sprout.
Growing because I matter
Sometimes we feel like our lives are standing still,
but we are far from motionless
I matter
I matter
I matter

You are Enough

We are always working on ourselves because
who we are doesn't feel authentic
We don't believe that people see the best parts of us
So, we are constantly trying to become an ideal that doesn't
exist.
Because at the core, we don't think what we portray is
honest.
But you are enough.
You don't have to be the best version of yourself.
Who you are and what you do now is perfect.
You are enough
Embody it.

Romance starts with You

Time waits upon your breath,
Swept into your mural of wild stories.
Yielded in the slow burn of midnight's
youthful blue and crescent stir of light.
Time contemplates racing forward, excited and
Joyous, for the beauty you will unveil,
Hidden in the glittering silk facade of your fears
Time waits upon your breath,
Watching you tread in the fluxes of the past
Reading the pages of your
romance, wondering if you ever
got the love you wanted?

GODS AND PEOPLE

We are the tranquil blue embodiment of life,
and a part of a society that tells us to feel both numb and
alive.
Today we are taller than the dreams beneath us.
We are omniscient,
powerful,
perspectives of beings.
We are a higher design.
Rise
Gods of poetry, remnants of people

My trauma.

It wasn't necessarily pain, just a part of my story that I had thrown in the back of the attic, collecting dust beneath the pieces and floorboard of who I once was. It is not that it's surreal; it's that I lived it and somehow survived to look back. That is why these tears matter. It is proof that God gave me the will to bend light and not become splinters in the fractures. It shows how hard and how brave I was, I am, and I will be, a marker of all things to come—an absolute. It teaches me that resilience is in the mind if one seeks the light. Love is but a show, a phantom of decisions you made in a moment, a spark of feeling that turned the night to ember glows.

So, when we choose to love and kindness every day, we make it infinite. When I use the word "my" in front of trauma, it is ownership, an emblem, a pride of a chapter I have run through, like gliding across a continuum of ice.

I hold these truths to be self-evident, my power, my ego, my right to freedom, on the pursuit of peace. A beautiful cycle to a story that I will get to say to my children; one day, when I grow old, I survived.

MEANINGS

It was hard for me to understand the limitations of meaning. So, I forgave myself for letting you mean the world to me when I got nothing in return.

Chemical War

We burn with resentment (fuel)
Towards the things we never
had enough of (oxygen)
Sometimes we break, like the high
 tempos and melodies on a
 music sheet(heat).
Then we swell, burning cold to the core.
We are breathing while hurting;
empty mantras in the rain;
fiery hail (comets).

What's Your Dream Job?

"I do not dream about labor,
I dream about meaning something."

-Eli & Shay

A collection of thoughts you may relate to

Taking off my make-up, going natural, and smiling was never the problem. However, being vulnerable, healing my trauma, and admitting I was not ready for love felt like swimming with sharks while bleeding.

I went deep enough to trace the scars of your trauma, blending into the stitches of your pain.
I made your healing mine, bellowing in the lonely embers of your air because I thought that's what love was. A sexual experience of worship, lucid and ritualistic as I became everything you needed, I became midnight in the understanding of you. My healing came not from running you down but from standing up. See, baby, we were never darkness; I just hid my moonlight.

When we are kids, we play make-believe; we create worlds and structures for our amusement.
We slay dragons, fight demons, pretend to be heroes, and maybe even kiss a Prince. When we grow up and do this, it is called Dissociation, Anxiety/Depression, and toxic relationships. I guess that is why I want to be a child forever.

Holding Space for Feelings

I hold this space for you, like a friend saving a seat at the movies.
I fight for this place, like road rage in a parking lot.
I hold you closer than arms, and heart, pressed against the cages of what I am afraid to show.
I hold you like purpose holds the fine intricate granite of your thoughts.
I hold you like pursed lips and clenched teeth.
I held you like flowers and reefs before the sea.
A ceremony to show you how much you mattered at the moment.
Then I let you go

Despite It.

Some of us are waiting to feel,
Some of us are waiting for motivation
Or the perfect moment,
But I need to tell you to do it despite what you feel or have,
Look at it this way
despite what they told you, you have overcome
Despite how they treated and hurt you, you still radiate love
Despite how hard your circumstances are, you still believe
in yourself
and something greater than this moment.
Despite what you believe, you still are better
Despite your limitation, you are winning the race
Life present obstacles, and despite them, you thrive
So, do it right now!
Good things are their way!

Losing Ourselves

The more I beg you to see my value,
the more it diminishes.
Fires from afar possess this beautiful, hypnotic allure,
like glowing fairies dancing on mountains,
but in person, they burn.

Completing Our Journey

Someone asked me,
"How are you so positive?"
And my answer was this:

Yesterday,
I felt a lump under my arm, and it dawned upon me
how fragile life is, like dandelions in the wind.
So here I was touching the absolute concrete truth,
it felt tiny, jaded, and smooth, with a hard center.
One day I will die.

One day I will not open my eyes and experience the joy of
a fresh-squeezed morning as the tangerine sun cascades
across my cheeks. I will not smell the sweet cinnamon buns
from the corner café, and I will not hear the wonders of the
world whistle and speak to me, the way the ocean does
when it roars against the rocks. One day I will not know the
experience of touch, language or see the expression of love
through murals of music that echo in the chambers of my
heart.

Knowing this, I laughed!
Joy leaked from the crevices of my grin, cracking my face
as the light in my eyes glowed.

I don't think you understand, the liberation!

I will die, I will die, but in this very infinite and precious
moment, I will live. And like sweetness, I will stretch my

existence like the stars across the endless vast sky, living each moment in God's graces, not waiting for life to cycle again.

Unequivocal

You do not deserve the laughter I conjure because the roots were a pain.

You did not dig, and you did not pull, you did not burry, or scream tears of hurt at night. You did not ache in the serrated edged thorns of loneliness. My beauty did not bloom for your aesthetic liking.

Everything you take so casually is part of an intricate force; every molecule of energy, every motion, and entropy, is not your respite! It cost me my peace. That price is too high for someone who does not care.

I am sorry it is not even enough for someone who wants to try to care.

Parts of me died to become a wildflower. If you knew the sacrifices I made, you would water yours.

Conversations with my inner child

Hello sweetheart,
Be gentle, be sweet, and be kind.
I have seen how you grow,
Your beauty knows no limitations.
Your strength inspires yourself.
Just hold on to who you are.
Pray and seek God because he will always
protect you.
You are the center of love, and you are
everything the world needs.

Always reaching

I will be first to admit,
I'm a little fucked up because I'm always reaching,
for that simplified version of us.
The idea of… an inkling to give justification to the cause
of…
The dust that drifts between the empty and the fragments of
My perspective looks up to you like the stars, which means
that you will always be in a higher position. That's how
much I care!
I am always reaching for you, slipping between the loose
grasp of your will; you slid through my heart like rivers.
You move the way time does, a constant flux of relativity.
Because you left me, not once but in every person I have
met after. A digression so far, the stars call it a line that
never touches.

So meanwhile, I reach for love; please tell me that you are
in a fixed position, an absolute, a state of philosophical
existence, a dimension that is not invisible.
So, I do not have to lose, bruise, and find through hurt and
time that you are emotionally unavailable like the silver
seams between your heart and mind.
Because I am reaching for your love
Mom…please love me.

If I am alone, what will happen?

Emotional Drug Addict

I get high off my need for validation,
I get low from the reality of expectations.
I hit you late at night, like one hit to the
vein, so I feel alright.
Then in the morning, I suffer from withdrawals,
the irony is you are not my reason,
I am addicted to the feeling of being needed.
These are the cycles of disfunction,
The screams
The "I need you, but you don't need me."
Hate the feeling of loneliness, so I let you own me.
Drinking bitter, burning regret, losing time,
but no one wants to be sober
because, at my worst, I feel high.

Ferris Wheel

Today, I heard you.
Perhaps we're all the same.
A silent sanctuary against the flooding

The coast of our hearts, beating to be heard
Perhaps, life treats us like a Ferris Wheel if we allow it
Slow, gentle creeks, flashing colors, the facade,
the pixilated splendor and heights that take us out of
perspective.

And suddenly, you are moving, desperate to reach the top.
Because if you get there,
it will all make sense.

However, sometimes we reach the top.
Then we get to see a different perspective as we watch the
people below.
The way they live, the way they laugh like thunder rolling
on mountains.
The way they dream so peacefully and coquettishly.
The way they smile, joy flowing so freely like rivers of
honey.

We notice they are kind; they are love, an equilibrium.

And now we want that too.

I think we want the God of small things to make
infinitesimal changes in our life, just enough to be
comfortable, just enough to say we matter, yet not brave
enough to leave the Ferris Wheel.

So, the Ferris wheel goes on...a perpetual circle of idealism versus self.

Round and round (hate, hurt, blame, etc...)

Up and down (euphoria, depression)

Moving. (Lost)

Yet we are no closer to what we need; empty like
dust between the space and stars.
Now, we want God,
because all along he was
time.

Aftertaste

If when you leave, all I taste is your bitter,
Spitting your name out like salt on Tequila,
Pungent and sour.
If when you leave, all I feel is empty, where beautiful
should fill.
If when you go, all I see is darkness and landfills of waste.
If when you leave, the flames of our charred hearts disperse
into the ether,
and silver linings burst
between the clouds.
Glowing with the love I have found in myself
Then I know I will have made the best decision I could
To rid me of your aftertaste.
You were never the best part of me; I know
 because I can taste you on my tongue.

To My Sensitive People

You put all the beautiful parts of yourself; first, you do not hide,
And you lay your heart bare, filled with empathy and compassion for the things most.
People are too busy to see. You greet the dawn with sparkling eyes and winter with a warmth that makes the trees shiver. You are an element of nature, alchemy of grace, a dealer of kindness, and a retrograde. Like the wind, everyone goes through you, but only you possess the power to pick yourself up again. You hurt when they do because, like stars, you know the strength of a constellation and how beautiful they shine. You love like a stranger, tethered without intentions, knowing that all you give is enough, and you don't need any payments.
Free-falling from heaven just to feel the chase. Your heart is greater than the sea, with the capacity to love infinitely yet so fragile and easy to break.
So next time some say you are too sensitive,
Say thank you because all it means is you are brave enough to feel...

To My Sensitive People (Part 2)

You are love without measure, and some people will try to limit and crush you.

You must have a sense of self-preservation, which does not necessarily mean you have to be selfish or limit your love. Self- preservation is the ability to rest and understand that some people who touch you are poison. Listen to what your body and mind tell you, and know that you must come first. Sinking to the bottom of the sea to save someone is still drowning, standing on the ledge to balance someone else is still falling. Breaking a boundary to help is still leaving you susceptible to breaking yourself. Sometimes the most extraordinary form of love you can give someone is saying no. It is not our job to save anyone, and it is our job to exist so people can see an extraordinary and healthy version of us. Love is just a decision, not a feeling, and we must decide that we are worth it.

I am not a poet.

Most nights, I quiver, disheveled fragments.
I elude into the night.
Entropy, a gradual shift in energy
I orbit, an unrequited foreigner.
Stick my tongue out!
Taste the promises I designed.
Ostensibly, I stand out.
I am motion,
infinitesimal hegemony.
Equanimity.

To the Next Person That Enters My Life.

Chow, mi nombre es Joyce.
I have this thing.
When people enter my life, I turn into a puppy.
Bright Bourbon sparkling eyes and a broad set of teeth that
cage constant airy laughter.
When you meet me, I'll have a newfound excitement and
energy,
and I'll try my very best to make you feel how loved
I wish I could be.
How loved I hope I could be.

Don't worry; I won't pee in your shoe,
But I'll be the stain in your heart,
you won't forget.

I love when the morning light hits my face,
or when I wake up happy.
It's the brightest thoughts that create a horizon.
I cry a lot,
I'm not sad; I just feel the world all in one heart.
It's just an expression of how beautiful God is.

I've been hurt before, like the lines against a fault. So
please excuse the wall I have.
Time will erode it; like Jericho, it will come tumbling
down.

When I'm at my worst,
I'll love you softly.
When I'm at my best,

you'll feel.

I crack my knuckles and have poor eye contact, and humor
is my mask.
My voice shakes when I'm upset or when it's trying to
keep up with the tempo of my heart.
My sister says it gets high when I like someone.

My favorite thing to say is *breathing me in*.
We were once dust until life formed.
That's why I'm careful who I kiss or touch.
We are matter, kinetic energy, depth, a collective of higher
design.
A thought is reaching for love.
Remnants on a celestial sphere.
Emotions represent fragments of God
We make meaning.

Did I mention I ramble?
Anyways,

If I even remotely like you as a person,
I promise to be the green lights, the ink of a poet, the filling
to your emptiness.
I promise to learn with you as time mentors us. I want
what you want,
to be heard,
valued
and understood.
Deeply
So, uh, yeah *por favor quédate?*
To the next person who enters my life

(Will you please stay?)

Paper Made People

Assembled in the thoughts, you shaped,
You formed me.
Interacting with existing materials,
put me together piece by piece.
I absorbed your indelicate dictation,
the words you yelled when I was a blank slate.
The way you see me makes me feel thinner than paper,
So, I rip apart, and you can reassemble me.
I am a montage of

"You are...."
"You should...."
"What's your label?"

Pressed and permeated by different experiences,
unraveling in the abstract
Because people are motivated by feeling.
We create visually pleasing dynamics
without removing fragments.
A line of beauty in a contemporary frame
When all I want is to be myself,
but you attach so much madness to meaning.
Washing away the heaviness of words off my back
Because beauty is more than your reason.
I don't want to be what society made,
paper collages.

Painting You

You were wary of the darkness,
So, I showed you an oil painting
"Impression, Sunrise" by Claude Monet
I asked if you saw the feelings between the strokes,
The invisible softness that traces the formless canvas?
The variants of light and the abstract colors that playful
bleed between
our understandings...
You said you noticed the sun and its reflection on the
water,
you paid more attention to the dark silhouettes and how
 Even the lack of color brought more attention to its beauty.
You pointed out how there were no clear boundaries
between the land and
the sky, but a depth of beauty that goes beyond form.
I asked what you loved the most about this painting, and
you said there is a stillness between the hues, a beating
heart telling secrets in the misty fog.
A reverence for love and appreciation for nature,
Thoughts anchored in the past playing with the movement
of color. The sun settles with love and content, drawing
forth everything simple towards it.
You observed that the absence of light is what gives this
piece its power and beauty,
 a movement, nothing is still…."
It demands a natural state of acceptance.

You were wary of your darkness, so I showed you a
painting.

Friendship in Hard Times

We are building in the afterthoughts of napalm skies and quiet lines—soft clay within our hands, dreams, and empathy are woven into our decisions. The world tilts on its axis, spinning in a conglomerate of voices and echoes, and somehow, I heard you through the glass. Who knew our soft melodies and memories would lead to friendship?

I lost days between the waste of resentment, and in one change of an instant, you gave life back to me. You were just a series of moments that love let us hold, filling the nights with laughter, good food, and the type of stains that don't come out readily.

You gave me a harness to sanity, a smile that breaks the darkness apart and made my worst days mean. You are my poetry, and the most beautiful lines blush red from your heart.

It is crazy how every stranger we meet holds the possibility of a version of us, but not of knowing, of becoming. When it is hard to accept the love I've kept from myself, you gently stored it for me.

I know we will last deep in the sediments, holding on to all the scars and tattoos that life has given us, keeper of secrets. It's simply extraordinary to meet a heart that beats even louder, to find someone bold enough to travel without any sense of direction, kind enough to spot you, and creative enough to paint a new picture past our perspective.

We are the rings of a tree, our friendship only becomes more profound with time, and I am grateful to have you.

Beacon of Light (God's promise to Us)

Hope will always find you,
Through every fuliginous fragmented, light loss moment
It will always find you, even if I must walk upon the sun
Even when my hands are tied to my heart, I will see you in
every ascension to meaning.
I will find you in the silence because I feel the gravel of
your pain against the soot burned skies.
I will always find you even if I run to the end of obsolete. I
will love you past your faults because what's breaking is
diamonds.
I will try venter into the somber grotto of your wild.
I will fight the imaginary, caliginous voids of depravity and
bring you back to life! I will find you in the measures of
love, oscillating in the weight of what it means to be a poet.
I promise I will always find you, even when the world
deconstructs itself, even when you are hurting to be loved,
even when your root aches from the shards of being
broken.
Even as you unravel, hope will find you in the static of
where freedom plays, and muse is just another word for
self. I know I will find you because you rest your beacon in
settlement of becoming.

The Lord said, "Let there be light…" and there was.

Moon Baby

Softly we strummed in her milky silk,
Frolicking in the abstract,
Stumbling through the lunar sea,
wading through our worries.
Then time brought upon change and change.
Molded into craters
Big monstrous holes, where people touched
Now to persevere ourselves, we eclipse,
wanting to be full again.

Purpose and Pursuit

So many of us are racing towards the idea of purpose. We see it as a name tag that identifies us, and we become frustrated when we cannot find something that we are good at. We often mistake wanting to feel alive again as purpose, but I do not believe purpose is a feeling of singularity. I believe the purpose is to find a deeper version of yourself; time and time again, memories and experiences shape how you think and interact.

So, if you are looking for a purpose...

I would say slow down and enjoy the moments between your dreams and finding you. Not knowing who you do not make you worthless; it makes you valuable to an infinite stream of possibilities.

I wrote this for you

When you woke up this morning,
did you know people's spirits rose?
At the thought of seeing you?
Did you know that eternity wouldn't?
Last without you?
It listens to the tempo of your passions,
waiting for the sky realm to liberate
the sails of beauty's womb.
Like natural hot springs, your soothing blue,
sparking aurora was the minerals they
needed to feel alive again.
Did you know that when the sun sets?
And draws the darken quivers of the earth back,
receding behind pillowy clouds.
It is a sign of submission.
It was made to worship your light.

Do you know how much you matter?

The Giver

I left my thoughts behind,
all the heavy, fixed variables that could not be changed.
Softly unpacking between the waves, my burdens left my
veins.
Eyes laid upon the blue bobbing in the gentle currents,
bones warmed in the sun,
letting the swirls cradle me.
drawn to the past, I opened the sails of my heart,
so it could stretch towards the omniscient burn of light.
Freedom traced my curves until it outlined a path past my
plight.
Then I started to trust myself, to flow in the connectivity of
limitless unrestraint.
I am the wind; I pushed my courage forward, treading in
the sublime, wisp and airy.
Expression in my blood, expanding across the vast open,
until I was floating.
Between space.
If you ask me how I survived,
I will say I am a giver,
who gave it all away.

Lost Lover

The stars could never quite align
as they cascaded in the soot of midnight.
Lost in the space where heaven matters.
Unrequited, lonely travelers suspended in your remnants.
Crying softly for gravity to pull me to you again,
but all I hear are the echoes of an infinite continuum.

Now God watches you wander across the elements,
In the mane of her stratosphere.
Nostalgic of a time when you moved the planets to
hold me close until we collapsed into ourselves.
Sometimes I still feel the rift of your bright
celestial energy.

You were the ambit of everything I wanted.

Being Human

Being human means feeling confident
and insecure at the same time.
Brave and powerful, and yet vulnerable
to the little things.

But I enjoy the part of being human
that means *love.*

The most beautiful things grow from dark spaces,
The most beautiful things grow from dark places,
The most beautiful things grow inside.

illustration

by: Tanya Antusenok

Everything in the Light

These past years have been incredibly hard on everyone. We have lost so many good souls, and now there are not just empty rooms in our homes but also our hearts. We've been slowly picking up the pieces, and time has been moving forward without us. So many of us are struggling to be okay when we are barely breaking the surface. I wanted to let you know; I hear your cries at night; I feel the lonely, aching parts you hide with powdered foundation and a happy little pill that ironically makes you feels far from joy. You are not alone. I wrote this to encourage you to keep going and know that you will be okay without a doubt. So, congratulate yourself on how brave and strong you have been, even as you crumble. The light is breaking behind those gloomy, dense, dark clouds. Happiness and peace are only a breath away. Take comfort in knowing you are *Everything the Light Touches.*

And when you are ready, use this light to touch someone else.

Extra (Sensual Poem)

On ocean nights, your fingers erect
summer's storm.
Warm, grainy sands sink beneath your,
soft, delicious compromise.
Balmy whispers reverberate in the palm of night,
when your eyes refract luminescent streaks of
glowing fires.
Humid betrayals cascade off your ripples
Content in your sighs, connective currents.
You are the tempo
as we float.
Praying to be shipwrecked,
Azul waves.

To My Favorite McGraw

I will not forget the light you poured into me when I was at my whisp. You laughed at my wit and encouraged me to be a comedian. I told you I would be a writer, and you said to do both! I will not forget your grace and the way you judged all my quizzes. You allowed me to be, me, never harsh or critical. You laughed at my choices in dessert and found it funny when I had to run to the altar and pray for; you know what....

Regardless of my wayward decisions, you embodied me like family and always held kindness for me in your office, along with historical facts and many exciting stories about your life.

The sound of your belly-aching laughter still echoes through the halls, and so does the impression God gives to you, for me. You were a part of my prayers when I asked God to guide me and show me my light.

It might seem over the top, but what people remember the most in life is the way you made them feel, and you made me feel empowered and extraordinary! So, thank you for being a wonderful human, good friend, and exceptional educator.

*A special note to my teachers.

The best part of my journey has been learning from you.

I don't know who I'd be if I didn't walk into Stauffer Hall

and immerse myself in the madness of words. Part of my

happiness consistently involves tea, classic literature, over-

analyzing everything, and creating stories I am proud of.

Writing has always been deeply personal because I

struggled to speak and read as a child. Having a learning

disability was like having a misspelled tattoo across my

forehead. Awkward, humiliating, and always prone to

someone's insensitive comment, *"You should get that*

fixed." Although several people worried about me at times

(me included), this isn't a sob story. It is about the

moments after..., and I am happy to say I never gave up. I

worked hard and appreciated all the people who worked

hard with me. I won't forget the cardio I did every time I

walked up the stairs to the language department to have

lunch with my favorite teacher, and I won't forget your encouragement, the challenges, the brute honesty, and the long nights with SparkNotes.

My teachers inspired me to be *Thoreau* and love the *Lawrence* in me. Others accepted my non-S.D.Stories, dry satire, and let me make fun of their cooking skills. The extraordinary ones taught me about medieval literature and how grace is the most effective form of chivalry. I fell in love with Shakespeare's sonnets, but the teacher who taught that class showed me the depth of love and life beyond prose. *Sometimes, love is an ever-present assurance that we will be okay.*

Some teachers were quiet but phenomenal and taught me that American literature is profound because their voices reflect a movement. A good teacher stood on tables to display great literary angst and educated me on phallic symbols. Another educator who gave me Dickens, Morrison, Vonnegut, *Waugh,* and others gave me PTSD from throwing sticks at me. But most of all, each professor taught me the importance of love, community, and support as a vital part of education. They taught me the importance of living my dream. They told me to keep writing not because I was good but because they believed in me. The power of words holds the same strength as seeds. They invested in my health, guarded my mental, and slowed down so I could catch up when life was not gentle. Now I am growing into the writer they have always seen.

So, thank you.

I dedicated myself to all the incredible teachers that were a part of my education.

*Special thanks to Mrs. Hendrix, my high school friend. You were the first person to pour light into my dreams. You told me, *"You're going to be a great author, and I can't wait to read your books!"*

Follow and Support Me on Social Media

Tik Tok @JoycetheSunbeam

Instagram @sun_beambabies

Email @joycewritely.orb@gmail.com

Also, look out for some more amazing reads coming to Amazon 2021-2022!

Sex Therapy- Erotica

Float- Young Adult-Novel

The Way We Love- Coming of Age Novel

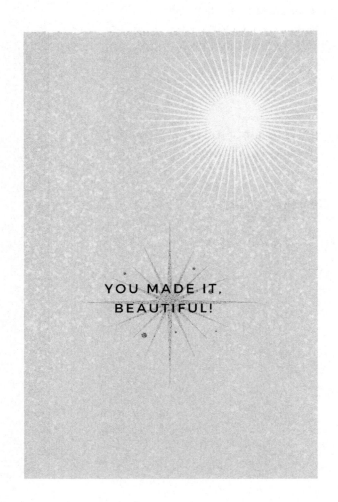

YOU MADE IT,
BEAUTIFUL!

Printed in Great Britain
by Amazon

82674373R00088